Raped by Man, Saved by God

Tamar Village

authorHOUSE

AuthorHouse™
1663 Liberty Drive
Bloomington, IN 47403
www.authorhouse.com
Phone: 1 (800) 839-8640

© 2018 Tamar Village. All rights reserved.

No part of this book may be reproduced, stored in a retrieval system, or transmitted by any means without the written permission of the author.

Published by AuthorHouse 03/12/2018

ISBN: 978-1-5462-3304-6 (sc)
ISBN: 978-1-5462-3302-2 (hc)
ISBN: 978-1-5462-3303-9 (e)

Library of Congress Control Number: 2018903167

Print information available on the last page.

Any people depicted in stock imagery provided by Getty Images are models, and such images are being used for illustrative purposes only.
Certain stock imagery © Getty Images.

This book is printed on acid-free paper.

Because of the dynamic nature of the Internet, any web addresses or links contained in this book may have changed since publication and may no longer be valid. *The views expressed in this work are solely those of the author and do not necessarily reflect the views of the publisher, and the publisher hereby disclaims any responsibility for them.*

Contents

Chapter 1 Left Behind 1

Chapter 2 The Church 13

Chapter 3 The Railroad Track 19

Chapter 4 Danger in the House 23

Chapter 5 School Days 27

Chapter 6 The Victim 31

Chapter 7 Two Angels 39

Chapter 8 The Pain Within 45

Chapter 9 Depression 51

Chapter 10 The Detectives 55

Chapter 11 Leaving Home 61

Chapter 12 The Child Within 69

Chapter 13 The Birth 75

Chapter 14 The Trial 87

Chapter 15 The Verdict 97

I dedicate this book back to God, who allowed it
to be birthed. I thank Him for saving my life.
This book is also dedicated to all
those who are victims of rape,
and abuse. Maybe you have never told
anyone, or maybe you are
ashamed and the pain is still there.
We must forgive and move
on, forgetting those things which are behind us, we press
forward.
The main reason I wrote this book, is to let
you know that you can overcome any adversity
in your life by trusting in God and
putting him first.

First and foremost, I thank God for his boldness, grace and mercy for allowing me to share my life with you. Thanks to those who edited this book and believed in my dreams. Thanks to my parents who raised me and taught me to love and depend on God. To the late Bishop, who taught me to always put God first. To my biological sisters, to my brother and my adopted sister, for supporting me through the years. Special thanks to all my other friends and co-workers who have stood by me over the years. A very special thank you to all those who contributed financially. Thank you for your support and believing I have a story worth sharing. May your return be one thousand fold.

To my Pastor, for feeding me the Word of God that I may meditate in it day and night and have good success. Finally, to my family, my daughter and three sons whom I love dearly.
To God be the glory!

Chapter 1

Left Behind

Danger is all around us but we have no warning signs to let us know from what direction it will come. Perhaps, it is at your house or your school. It could be next door or in the social club. It could be your friend, sister, brother, father or mother. Always be careful. Stop and beware that danger may be ahead. We never expect anything bad to happen to us, but every person possesses a good side and a bad side. It's what direction you take in life. Are you going in the right direction or the wrong direction? I was going in the right direction. However, danger was just ahead and waiting in the path to attack the first victim in sight. You guessed right.....I was that victim.

I would like to return to my childhood. It was the month of July and extremely hot, my mother was calling a taxi to come and get us. She had packed our clothes and seemed to be very nervous. There was a look of confusion on her face and I wondered where we were going and if she was making the right decision. My mother had three girls, my oldest sister Annabella, she was short, of fair complexion and had long beautiful hair. Also, there was myself and my baby sister Selma, whom we nicknamed "Red" because she was light skinned and had medium length sandy red hair. I do not remember very much of my childhood. However, I do remember not being very happy. We were always moving from place to place, never living in the same place for any long period of time. The summer days and nights were hot and long. The only relief we had was the fan blowing cool air to stop the heat wave. I guess my mother had done the very best she could, being a single mom and trying to make ends meet.

The sun's heated rays were burning into the taxicab. The air conditioner must have been broken, because the taxi driver's face was all wet. Sweat was dripping from his face. He was a tall and slender man. He never smiled or said much. My mother was sitting in the front seat and my two sisters and I were sitting in the back. My mom appeared to be tired and looked as if she needed some rest. As I looked down at my sisters, they were fast asleep. I laid my sister's head in my lap so that she could sleep more comfortably. She had very beautiful hair and as I stroked her hair, I looked out of the window, still confused. I heard my mother tell the cab driver this was our stop, to pull over and wait; she would be right back.

As I looked out of the window, I saw a fair skinned lady waving. She wore a pink housedress and her smile was as warm the Summer day. My mother exchanged words with the her and started to walk back towards the cab. The cab driver unloaded the trunk with our suitcases, to give to the lady in the pink housedress. I had so many questions, and no one to answer them, like where were we going, who was this lady and why was my mother bringing us here? My mother awakened my sisters and carried the youngest one in her arms. She told me to get out of the car, when I got out of the car, I saw chickens and roosters running everywhere in the yard. One of the animals ran towards me, my heart began to pound and I ran towards my mother, crying and begging her for help.

My mother was about to leave so she kept walking towards the cab, not even looking back. I ran after my mother but the lady held me and told me not to cry and said that everything would be all right. As the car drove off I felt lost and all alone. My sisters and I looked at each other as if to ask where is mother going and when will she come back to get us? I wanted to be strong for my sisters, so I held back the tears and suppressed the hurt and pain I felt about our mother leaving. I wondered "how could a mother leave her own children?" Perhaps she had to work and we would be in the way, or maybe she was having a hard time making it with three children. I tried to understand what was going on however, there were no answers to my questions.

My sisters cried and I tried to comfort them because I now felt responsible for their safety. I felt that I had to be the maternal figure for them. I told them that everything would be all right and not to worry. The lady stood looking at me and just smiled and said "you are right, with the help of the

Good Master, I will take care of you and your sisters." As we stood looking and hoping that my mother would change her mind and come back for us, tears of sadness and pain were rolling down my face. My sisters cried so much that they fell asleep.

The lady introduced herself as Mrs. Hunter and told us that we would be living with her and her husband. Ms. Hunter was short and kind of heavy set. Mr. Hunter was a short and stocky man, who would always rub his mustache. He was not a man of many words.

As we entered the small white cinder block house, a space heater was in the living room along with a small couch and a green high back chair. There was also a pot belly stove in the middle of the living room used to help heat the house. There were pictures on the wall of a white man, with long hair. Mrs. Hunter later told me that it was Jesus, the son of God. I really did not know who God was. She told us that she would teach us about Him later on. I observed the house and noticed the curtains were made out of plastic, with lots of flowers in all colors. I saw a large washtub that was used for washing clothes. She explained to me that she made lye soap and that one day she would teach me how to do that too. The kitchen was very small and the sink had a wash pan for washing dishes. We did not have an inside bathroom, instead we had an outhouse. There were two bedrooms; my sisters and I had to share the same bed. We did not mind because we wanted to be together. We promised each other that we would never leave each other.

Outside Mr. Hunter had a garden with plenty of food to eat....tomatoes, collards, bell peppers, potatoes, and cabbage. We would sometimes help Mr. Hunter cultivate his garden, plowing and planting the seeds for the next season. We always heard them say we should live off the land that God gave us and we would never be hungry. The only foods we had to purchase were dairy products and different types of meat, with the exception of chicken, which they raised. When we had chicken for dinner, they would get the chicken from the chicken coop. Mrs. Hunter would make delicious homemade bread for us. When we sat down to eat Mr. Hunter would lead the grace and we would repeat after him.

Some days Mrs. Hunter would cook late in the evenings. During those times I felt like a bird searching for food and I would eat from the various fruits trees planted in the yard. We had a walnut tree, peach tree, apple tree, plum tree grape vines and blackberries. My sisters and I would hit the trees and the fruits would fall off and we would eat them until Mrs. Hunter finished cooking. Life was not bad for us, Mr. and Mrs. Hunter made us feel that we were so rich that we never knew we were poor. I felt very blessed living with them because they raised and loved us as if we were their very own children. God truly supplied all of our needs. We had a place to live, food to eat, and clothes to wear. God had a purpose for our lives. We wanted our mother to raise us however, God predestined Mr. and Mrs. Hunter to raise us and they became known to us as Ma' and Da'. We became a real family with two parents as opposed to just one. God always knows the future and what the outcome will be.

We later learned that our mother was in New York and had found a job there. She would send us clothes and money from time to time to help Ma' and Da' with expenses. Sometimes our mother would send us a Christmas box. It was a very exciting time for us, as we all wondered what was in the box, but we could not open it until Christmas.

I liked Da' because he was a man of few words, but he had authority and when he spoke, we all listened. Da' paid all of the bills and made sure we were all well fed. He was a very smart man. We had an outside toilet and I used to dream that snakes could come up and harm us. When Da' finally decided to build a bathroom onto our house we were thrilled. There would be no more going outside in the middle of the night or in the cold to use the bathroom. Da' could build anything he put his hands on. He was a very smart man and worked downtown at the Prince Charles Hotel in the engineering department, where he repaired the heating system and made sure that it worked properly. He would catch the bus back and forth to work until he purchased a car. When he did purchase a car we were soooo... happy. Sometimes Ma' would not make bread so we would go to the bakery to purchase bread. We loved to ride in our new car so we would all just pile into the car to go to the bakery. Boy, life appeared to be getting better and better, our new found life was not as bad as we first thought it would be.

Later on we were introduced to Ma's daughter, Miss Moore. She was a short lady with bowed legs and beautiful jet black, wavy hair. She had a very small waist line, a nice figure and she loved to dip navy snuff. She had a young boy with her and Ma' introduced him as our older brother, James. I could not believe my ears. Our brother! How could this be? We never knew we had a brother, and why was he not with us? Still, so many questions, with very few answers. As I looked up at him, he smiled. His complexion was just like my two sisters and he was tall and skinny. I did not want to believe her. This had to be a lie, because my mother never told us we had a brother. My sisters and I stayed away from him, because we were not sure if this was true. We never said that much to him even though, he continuously acknowledged that he was, in fact our brother.

The time came when Ma' explained to us that we all had chores to do. I was responsible for cleaning the house, and washing the dishes. My sisters washed and ironed the clothes. Moore lived across the street from us, she would come over to braid our hair and help us around the house. We hated to get our hair pressed and curled. This meant that she would place the straightening comb on the stove and get it as hot as she could, then comb it through our hair. I was absolutely horrified when I saw the smoke coming from the hot comb. Sometimes Moore would burn my neck because I would jump from the heat of the comb. Moore said that I had bad hair, unlike my sister Annabella who had good hair, and did not need to have her hair pressed. Although, I often wished that I had hair like my sister. I figured hair was hair and I just needed a little more help with getting my hair straightened.

One cold winter day my chore was to wash clothes, I heated the water on the pot belly stove, carried it outside and poured it into the wash tub. I had to use lye soap and a wash-board to clean our clothes. The lye soap did not smell too good, but it did clean the clothes. Afterwards, I would hang them on the clothes lines to get dry.

While hanging the clothes on the line my hands became so cold and my lips begin to tremble. I hurried to get back in the house to get warm by the stove. I would rub my hands together to keep them warm, my eyes teared, and I had a snotty nose. Later Da' purchased a washing machine that had a clothes ringer on it. Once the clothes had been washed thoroughly, we then had to empty the soapy water out and run clean water into the machine to rinse, then we fed the clothes through the ringer, to ring out the excess water. Once again we were so elated that Da' saved us, from hand washing our clothes outside in the icy cold weather. The wash tub had now become history.

Moore would still come to help out by preparing our meals and making sure that we always had clean clothes to wear to school. Moore liked to drink and dance around the house. Sometimes, we would dance and have fun with her. She loved Marvin Gaye's song, "Let's Get it on", it was her favorite. She wore the flare type of skirts that swirled as she turned gracefully swaying to the music. She smoked Pall Mall cigarettes and made it look pretty cool to do so. One day Moore had a little too much to drink. Taking advantage of the situation, I snuck out and smoked a cigarette. I will never forget the severe coughing attack I had. I quickly realized that smoking was definitely not for me. I remember when there used to be a club located in front of our house which was called the "Juke Joint". Where different people would come to shoot pool, play cards, play music on the juke box and just hang out. It was later torn down.

Chapter 2

The Church

Ma' never used to drink but she did dip snuff, her favorite was Navy. To this very day she still dips snuff. Ma' was a church going woman and had accepted Christ in her life. She told us that we had to go to church, sing in the choir, and learn about God. When we did go to church it seemed like we went there each and every day. My sisters and I joined the choir; while singing songs of praise the Holy Spirit would come in and people would just shout all over the church. The Holy Spirit is the comforter that comes over you that has an amazing presence that warms your soul. It simple gives you the feelings of knowing that there is a God, how powerful he is, and what he can do for you without ever seeing him. Ma' would always say "Look up to the Master and everything will be all right." We were never allowed to listen to blues or rock-n-roll music in her presence, we could only listen to spiritual music. We also had to wear long dresses whether we were going to church or school. We did not get to wear pants at all, let alone to church. Ma' said that girls should never wear short dresses.

We learned so much about God, his son Jesus, how he died and when he rose from the grave. We were taught that we must have faith and believe that God is the beginning and the end. We also learned that we can never hide from God for he hears and sees everything we say and do. But if you sin, that God is so gracious and merciful that if we ask through repentance he will forgive us, for he is the only one who can forgive us of our sins.

I remember when there would be lightning during thunderstorms we would turn everything off in the house the TV and the stereo, we had to sit quietly and not say a word because ma' explained that the Lord was doing his work and we must not disturb him. After the rain storms, sometimes I would look up at the clouds and try to visualize shapes and images of the clouds. It seemed like the stars would be winking at me. When I looked up at the clouds I would sing and my sisters would think that I was crazy, but I did not care. I thanked God for the many blessings he had bestowed upon up us, the family he had given us, food to eat and clothes to wear.

Da' did not attend church at that time. Ma' would get up early on Sunday mornings to fix breakfast and send us up the railroad tracks to church. Our Pastor at Park's Chapel was Bishop E. A. Jackson. The church was a small, house-type sanctuary, with wooden chairs. We had a mourners bench, which is now called an altar. The old saints would tell us to go and get down on our knees and stay there until we repented of our sins. Sometimes my knees would get so tired, but we still had to keep calling out to God. There was no carpet on the floors during that time, the floors were made of wood. Sometimes we would be down on our needs so long that it felt like our knees had gone numb and we had no sensation left.

Baptismal day was the day when we had to go down to

the lake, located off of Raeford Road to be baptized. All candidates, both men and women who were getting baptized had to wear all white. This was the day that we were to be washed of all our sins. Depending on the season or the time of the year the water was refreshing when you were dipped under, but during the cooler months the water was really cold to the body. The church members would shout and praise the Lord as if we were having church right outside. Sometimes I would feel that God was in our presence when the older saints would dance right out of their shoes. We as children would laugh and think that they were crazy. I remember when I got baptized in the lake; with all the others I stood in line, scared, because I thought I might drown, but when I came out of the water I felt totally different. I was crying and praising God saying "Thank you Jesus, Thank you Jesus, Hallelujah," all at the same time. The lake is now dried up and every time I pass it I have pleasant thoughts of the time I got baptized there.

Later on Da' started going to church and gave his life to God. I know that he changed, because he stopped smoking and became a Deacon in our church. Ma' was happy and so were we. They always encouraged us, to have faith in God, not man. At night we would pray for guidance from God for the next day because he was our source of being and without him, where would we be?

Chapter 3

The Railroad Track

We were not allowed to be in adults conversations, children were to be seen and not heard. We never talked with the adults much unless they initiated the conversation with us first, otherwise you were considered as being fast and grown. They never discussed sex, making love, having children or our menstrual cycles. We actually had to learn the facts of life from our health classes at school or from what we could hear from the boys and girls in school. We were never given the opportunity to express ourselves to adults.

There was no violence, sex, profanity or nudity ever shown

that was shocking or tragic, it was never discussed, it was always kept hush-hush, only the adults were allowed to discuss it. There were very limited discussions or conversations of evil things that happened around us. We lived a sheltered life, where we were only exposed to discussing good things.

Today the world is different. We see sex on TV, and no one leaves anything for the imagination. Sex sells, people buy it, see it and sometimes take it. The way a person dresses or looks, should not determine that he or she is trying to provoke sexuality. The human psyche wants that which it cannot have, this is called control. During my childhood people helped each other and gave food when others did not have enough to eat. It didn't cost a lot to live. Ma' would sometimes work for Mr. Bennett and would earn about $9.00 per week, this was a lot of money back then. Ma'. would wash and iron Mr. Bennett's clothes for him. She would feed people that were hungry, even if she did not know them. I admired her for that, she had a very giving spirit. She would cook for the pastor and he would come for dinner after church on Sunday. We would have fried chicken, mashed potatoes, collard greens, tea and corn bread. He would laugh and rub his stomach as if to say he was to full. He would pray for God to bless us before he left to go home. We as children had to stay outside when the pastor was there. Ma' would always tell us to go outside to play. My sister and I would sit on the front porch and count the cars as they went by, she would say the next car is mine, we would take turns and the next car would be hers, sometimes we would get really nice cars and once in a while there would be raggedy cars that passed by. We would laugh, and have the best times of our lives.

We lived right beside the railroad track, so close that I would pray each and every night that the train would not fall on our house. We used to play on the railroad tracks, walking the rails to see who could walk the longest without falling off. One night the train was going so fast that the house shook and we heard a loud noise, it sounded like cars squealing. All of a sudden, the train came to a screeching halt. Shortly afterwards we heard sirens and people screaming and hollering. We jumped out of our beds and ran to the door. We went outside and heard people saying that the people in the car, were dead that the train had hit. Some people were saying that there were body parts founded up and down the railroad tracks. Tears came to my eyes, because the people in the car were dead and I was so sad. Ma' and Da' took us back in the house and told us to go back to bed and try to sleep. The next morning there appeared to be so much pain and sorrow in the air. We did not want to play on the tracks that day knowing that individuals had lost there lives there. I felt that their families must had been devastated over losing a loved one, where ever their families may have been located. We were afraid that we might see human body parts, like an arm, or a leg, or an eye. The clouds hung low and appeared to be very dark, and the sun did not shine for about a week. Ma' said she had heard a long time ago that a man died on the railroad tracks and people say up until this day, they can see the man at night holding a lantern in his hand trying to find his head. At night we were much too afraid to walk on the railroad tracks again.

Chapter 4

Danger in the House

We never had many friends because Ma' was very protective of us. She only wanted what was best for us and tried to protect us by keeping us close. However, danger can come into the house without us even being aware of its presence. One day Mr. Matthew, a friend of the family stopped by our house to visit. He was a tall, brown skin man with salt and pepper hair and a mustache. He was very friendly and comical and everyone liked him. I thought he always wanted to play with my older sister because she had very long hair and light skin and everyone thought she was very pretty. Sometimes, we would go into the kitchen and play cards. Mr. Matthew would hold my sister, in his lap and I can remember one particular time when a card fell on the floor. I crawled on the floor, under the table to search for the card and I noticed Mr. Matthew had his hands under my sister's dress. I was very shocked. I wanted to run and let Ma' know that danger was in our house, but I was too scared. From that point on I lost all respect for Mr. Matthew. He was very sneaky and whenever he came to visit, we would keep our distance from him. He never mentioned what happened, but he knew that I saw what he did. He always looked at me as if wondering whether I would tell his secret. I explained to my sister to never sit in his lap again.

A crime can happen and before you know it you are the victim. People used to be ashamed of there sexual orientation, but the closet doors are now wide open and no one tries to hide anymore. In the secular world it is called "Coming Out Of the Closet".

Biblically it is called, "Living In the Last Days." When we read the word of God, We read that God destroyed the towns of Sodom and Gomorrah because of the evil deed of the people. Women were lovers of women and men were lovers of men. Only Lot, his wife and daughters were saved. However, Lot's wife disobeyed God and looked back which caused her to lose her life.

Chapter 5

School Days

School was very important to me and even though I was not a smart or popular student, I always did my best. I did not have many clothes and I felt that sometimes the teachers had their favorites students. People tend to judge us by our outward appearance, before really getting to know the beautiful person on the inside. God made us all different and I thank him for that. What would the world be like if we were all the same?

School was a challenge for me. Ma' only had a third grade education so when we needed help, she would shy away and tell us stories about her school days; when she had to do her chores before going to school in the mornings and work in the cotton and tobacco fields after school. We had to help each other with our homework or figure it out on our own. Ma' would never check our homework, maybe it was because she did not know how. She never asked if we had any homework to do, she just worried about us doing our chores when we got home from school. When we arrived home, she would always have dinner on the table and would fix us lunch to take to school for the next day.

There was a girl during the time I attended Ferguson Elementary School, name Dawn who was mean to me. She was big, fat, and had huge lips and large feet. I was always afraid of her and I would run home after school so she would not torment me. I hated this girl and I wanted to fight her back, but I never did. Ma' always taught us to be nice to people and God would take care of the bad people. Dawn would always pull my hair because my braids were longer than hers and would make fun of me because I would bring a brown, greasy bag to school for lunch. Sometime I would eat my lunch walking to school. I wanted to eat in the cafeteria, but we could not afford it. Dawn dressed better than I did and would laugh at me because of the way I dressed.

One day at school we had a talent show. Since I could sing, I was going to be Diana Ross and my friends Shirley and Betty were the Supremes. Out of all the contestant we were the winners. My teacher Mr. Monroe, was very proud of us. As the winner of the competition we had to compete at another school. Ma' agreed that I could compete in the talent show, but the night of the show she changed her mind and would not allow me to be a part of the competition. I was so embarrassed. I was supposed to be Diana Ross and she said "No!!!" I wanted to run away. I thought she was the worst person on earth. Maybe she saw danger signs, which I was not aware of. It is often said that God will protect you and guide you. Now that I am saved, I know that he did because one of my friends who was in the group started drinking, taking drugs, dropped out of school, had a baby and a lot of other problems. I often wondered if I had been allowed to go to the talent show that night, if my life would had turned out like hers.

Chapter 6

The Victim

At the age of 14, something happened to me that made me feel as if my whole life was completely over. One day after school three of my friends and I were walking home on our usual route. We would laugh and talk about the things that had happened and how much fun we had in school that day. On the way home we would walk down Oharry Rd, at the University, we would then separate at Seabrook Park where my friends would go up the hill to the other side of the railroad tracks and I would walk down the tracks to get home. When we separated, I had to walk the rest of the way home alone, which was no big deal because I had always walked home this way before. Since we lived right beside the railroad track, this was a shortcut home for me. It was a dark, cloudy and misty day as I started home. I remember looking up at the sky thinking that since we started the day light saving time how it was getting dark earlier.

I had on my plaid coat that my mom had sent me from New York. As I walked along, I wondered what ms' was cooking for dinner. She always prepared meals that made you ask for more; she was such a wonderful cook. As I walked down the tracks, I begin to count the rocks on the track thinking of the games my sisters and I played. I decided I should walk a little faster, thinking that the rain might start before I could get home.

As I looked up, I noticed a man coming out of the path. He was walking towards me, but just as he passed me, he turned very fast, grabbed me by my neck, and threw me down to the ground. My heart begin to pound as if it was going to jump out of my chest, because I was so scared. All of a sudden, my books went everywhere. He grabbed me up then pushed and shoved me into the woods. I pleaded with him to let me go but he told me to "shut up and keep moving." Then he pushed me to the ground again and begin to drag me by my coat further into the woods. The ground was damp and the bushes were wet. The limbs and the thorns from the trees and bushes were painful rubbing up against my legs as they begin to bleed. He put the knife up to my throat and said, "I am going to rape you and if you try to get away I will kill you.". At that moment, I became traumatized, my voice left me and I could not say a word. I wanted to scream for help, but nothing would come out. My heart began to beat faster and faster. I started crying and managed to muffle, "stop, and please do not do this to me. He put his hand over my mouth, pressed the knife harder at my throat and whispered in my ear, "shut up, if you try to run I will kill you." I became the victim that had been captured by the enemy who was waiting to catch his prey. However, he did not care; he just kept repeating that he was going to kill me.

I trembled, with fear, closed my eyes and never said a word. In my mind I was crying out, "God, please help me. Where are you?" I wanted to fight back but I was too petrified. He had a horrible body odor and the smell of it made me sick.

He pulled my dress up, grabbed my panties and tore them off like a mad animal. He acted as if he was deranged. Tears began to roll down my face. I wanted to scream, "Please stop! Don't do this to me" but still not a sound would come out. As he unzipped his pants, I turned my head from side to side to keep from looking at him. I tried to keep my legs together but he violently pushed them apart. All I could do was pray in my mind, for God to help me. He began to touch me all over my body, feeling on my breast and rubbing his filthy, nasty hands up and down my legs. I despised the very thought of him touching me at all. This was absolutely the worst thing that I had ever experienced in my entire life. He was breathing hard and sweat was pouring from his face. He pushed his penis into my vagina with such force, I felt like my body has been ripped apart. The pain was so sharp and to the point of being unbearable. I laid there stiff as a board but he kept moaning and groaning making, guttural sounds that just made me nauseous. I do not know how long he held me there but it seemed like an eternity, all I wanted him to do was shut up and get off me so that this brutal act could end.

I was getting sick and felt like I wanted to vomit. I began

to wonder what he was going to do with me when he finished? I felt that my life was over and that he was going to kill me. I kept my eyes closed and kept praying for God to help me. I knew that God had to see what was happening to me, for he sits high and looks low and there is nothing you can hide from God. The rapist had taken a part of me that I could never retrieve again in life. He took a part of me that one day should have been my husband's. But, danger is everywhere. I learned in church that the enemy comes to kill, steal, and destroy. The enemy did steal a part of me that I can never retrieve again. And he did destroy my self-esteem.

In my demented state of mind of not knowing what was going to happen, I was still hoping and praying that God would intervene. I thought that if I was going to die that I would try to change my thinking process and concentrate on remembering the words of Psalm 91 "He that dwelleth in the secret place of the most high shall abide "under the shadow of the almighty. I will say of the Lord, He is my refuge and my fortress: my God; in him will I trust. Surely, he shall deliver thee from the snare of the fowler, and from the noisome pestilence. He shall cover thee with his feathers, and under his wings shall thou trust: his truth shall be thy shield and buckler. Thou shall not be afraid for the terror by night; nor for the arrow that flieth by day; Nor for the pestilence that walketh in darkness; nor for the destruction that wasteth at noonday. A thousand shall fall at thy side, and ten thousand at thy right hand; but it shall not come nigh thee. Only with thine eyes, shalt thou behold and see the reward of the wicked. Because thou hast made the Lord, which is my refuge, even the Most High, thy habitation; there shall no evil befall thee, neither shall any plague come nigh thy dwelling. For he shall give his angels charge over thee, to keep thee in all thy ways. They shall bear thee up in their hands, least thou dash thy foot against a stone. Thou shalt tread upon the lion and adder: the young lion and the dragon shalt thou trample under feet. Because he hath set his love upon me, therefore will I deliver him: I will set him on high, because he hath known my name. He shall call upon me, and I will answer him: I will be with him in trouble; I will deliver him, and honor him. With long life will I satisfy him, and show him my salvation."

I felt that I was very special to God that he loved me

dearly and I wondered why he would put me through such a traumatic experience. Ma' said that you should never question God but I felt like the God of my life had abandoned me.

Chapter 7

Two Angels

While lying there in a semi-subconscious state of mind I thought, I heard someone talking. Just as I opened my eyes, the rapist had a startled look on his face. He took his filthy hands, covered my mouth and whispered, "Don't make a sound; if you do I will kill you. He rolled off me, pulled up his pants, slid over into the bushes to try to hide so that no one could see him, then he got up and ran through the bushes. I know now that God heard me and sent his angels to protect me. He said in his word that he shall give his angels charge over thee to keep thee in all thy ways.

The enemy had taken my body, but God did not allow him

to take my mind and my life. I began to cry uncontrollably. I was so nervous that my whole body shook, like a tree with the cold wind blowing through it. My books were thrown everywhere, my coat was dirty and torn, my dress was literally ripped to pieces and I could not find my panties at all. My hair was all over my head, as if I had been in a fight. I tried to gather what I could of my belongings and get out of the woods. I was still crying because I could barely walk from the severe pain that I had in my vagina and I could feel something running down my legs but I was too afraid to look. As I came out of the woods, trying to get back to the tracks to go home I saw two men. They were coming out of the path and they looked at me as if to ask, "What happened to you?" I was still afraid because now I had to encounter two more men, wondering if they too would try to attack me. With tears rolling down my face I gained some inner strength and was able to ask them, if they could walk me home because I had just been attacked by a man in the woods and needed some help. They told me, "No" and just kept walking. I thought maybe they were afraid to help me because of perception or just simply not wanting to get involved. So I began walking

Raped by Man, Saved by God

home alone, crying, very hurt and afraid. Then I started to run as fast as I could. The rocks on the railroad tracks almost caused me to lose my balance. But, I kept running trying to get home, in my mind I thought, "What is that running down my legs," am I bleeding, am I going to die"? I began to get weaker and weaker my legs felt as if I was not going to make it. When I got closer to the house, the pain was too much for me to bear, I was totally exhausted and I wanted someone to help me.

When I got home, the insurance man was at my house because he came once a week to collect the monies for our life insurance policies. He looked at me as if he could not believe his eyes, at the same time Ma' was screaming at me, "Where have you been and what in the world happened to you; have you been in a fight; why are your clothes all dirty and wet?" The only words I could say were: "A man attacked me and did this to me".

When my brother heard my response, he quickly began to run down the railroad track as fast as he could to see if he could find the man. Ma' took me into the bathroom and told me to pull up my dress. As I pulled up my dress, we

Tamar Village

saw the blood running down my legs and I began to panic. Why was I bleeding? What was happening to me? Ma' & Da' began to ask me questions. I could not say a word and went into total shock.

Immediately, Ma' called the police. It did not take them long to arrive, but when they did come, it seemed as if there were police cars and blue lights flashing everywhere. They briefly asked Ma' what had happened. When she explained to them that I had been attacked by a man on the railroad tracks three of the policemen ran down the railroad tracks to try to find him. A short while later they returned with the rest of my books; they had also found my underwear and placed them in a plastic bag that they said this would be used as evidence.

Our neighbors came out of their houses and begin to investigate; asking questions as to what was going on and what had happened. As the people gathered and begin to whisper among themselves about the incident, I felt so embarrassed. All I could do was hold my head down and cry. I begin to think to myself that perhaps in some kind of way this was my fault. Maybe if I had never gone down

Raped by Man, Saved by God

the tracks by myself this would have never happened to me. I had walked the tracks previously almost every day and nothing like this had ever happened to me before. I began to blame myself for what happened. I questioned God and asked: "Lord why did this have to happen to me? I thought that you loved me."

Two detectives came to interview me, they asked me to give them all the details of what happened, they also wanted to know if I could identify the man, would I know his face again if I saw him and what was he wearing? I told them that I was walking home from school and I noticed a man coming out of the woods. I really did not pay much attention to the clothes he was wearing, but I did remember his face. I also informed the detectives of the two men that saw me as I was coming out of the bushes. One of them asked me, again to described how they looked and could I remember their faces? I assured the officer that if I saw the two men again I would definitely remember their faces. He said that during this investigation they would try to find the two men I described and ask them if they had seen the alleged suspect? He said they would ask the two men if they could identify the man and would they be willing to testify in court about what they saw?

The detectives advised ma' that we would need to go to the hospital to have a medical examination for rape victims. The detectives were going to take us to the hospital as we got in the police car the neighbors all looked and stared at us as if we were being hauled off to jail. As we drove away I felt so ashamed and so violated, like this has to be the worst thing that could happen to anyone. No one has the right to take what does not belong to them or what they have not been given permission to receive. It is just like stealing, someone robbing you for your possessions, but danger is everywhere. While we were riding in the police car there was an errie silence that fell in our presence and I began to cry again, Ma' held me tightly and kept telling me "don't worry baby, with the help of the good Lord everything is going to be alright."

Chapter 8

The Pain Within

When we arrived at the hospital, we went into the emergency room. The nurse at the sign-in desk saw that we were being escorted by the police and began to ask Ma' questions as to why we were there and the nature of the illness. Ma' explained to her that I had just been raped and needed to be examined by the doctor. Immediately, the nurse took me into the examination room and told me take off my clothes and change into the hospital grown that she was handing to me. As she turned to leave the room she said, "The doctor will be with you shortly."

I was left all alone in the examination room; it was a

small, cold and empty room with the exception of the exam table and medical instruments. I felt so lonely that I had no one to hold my hand to tell me that everything was going be alright, I did not know what to expect. I felt as though I had no support at all. I laid on the exam table and begin to cry, I became extremely nervous and my legs started to shake.

There was a tap on the door, a tall white man opened the door and walked in. He had on a long white jacket, dark hair and glasses with a large frame. He began to put on his gloves to examine me, he told me to try to relax, not to be afraid and that everything was going to be alright. Again, he asked me to try to relax because my legs were still shaking. I was sure the doctor had seen the blood because now I had bloodstains on the hospital grown. I had never been examined by a vaginal doctor before and I did not want him to touch me. I could not believe a male doctor had been sent in to examine me. I wanted a female doctor to check me, not a man! I had just been raped and I wanted to scream, "Please, don't touch me again!"

Suddenly, I had a flash back of the man who had just raped me. Tears began to run down my face. My legs trembled and my body shook like a tree. I kept hearing over and over again, "If you try to get away, I will kill you, I will kill you". I wanted to scream. The doctor said, "don't be afraid?" I have just been raped and you are telling me, "Don't be afraid?" I begin to shout in my mine "God, why me? You said that you would protect me and that you loved me; but, why me?" I was a virgin. I felt that I was being violated, all over again. I didn't want that man doctor to touch me. I just wanted to go home and wash, to get the smell and dirt off of me. I begin to build up anger, hate and a wrath for the man that had raped me and I wanted him to die for what he had done to me. Life just seemed like it was so unfair. I wondered why God: "would allow bad things happen to good people?" However, no one is ever exempt, from the possibility of evil.

After the doctor had examined me, he told me to get dressed. As I finished getting dressed, the nurse came in and told me to sit in the waiting area because she had to write an incident report about what had happened. When I came out the examination room Ma' was waiting for me. The doctor called Ma' into his office to talk to her. When she came out of the office I could tell that she had been crying. The police had been waiting outside and escorted us back to the car to take us home. It seemed like the coldest day of my life. My stomach ached and I felt sick and dirty. All I wanted was to take a bath and wash the pain away. As we rode in the police car going home the police informed us that the incident would be printed in the local newspaper, Ma' never said a word she just looked out the window and kept crying.

When we arrived home, the house seemed so cold and awfully quiet. I felt so ashamed, I wanted to go into a shell and never come out. I did not want to go back to school; because I knew, the kids would read the paper and be talking about me. Ma' had asked the police if they would not mention my name however, they didn't comply with her wishes. My name was printed in the paper the next day and I just knew that everybody knew what had happened to me. My sister looked at me and began to cry also just because I was crying. Yet, she did not realize the magnitude of what had happened to me. When I got in the house I immediately ran into the bathroom, locked the door, closed the curtains, turned on the shower and began to wash. I rubbed my body so hard that my skin began to burn and turn red. I sobbed and sat down in the bathtub as the shower water continued to run over my body. I never wanted to come out. I wanted to kill myself; I no longer had the desire to live. My mind began to play tricks on me and I kept hearing the voice of the man who had raped me whispering in my ear. I kept smelling the scent of his body and how awful it smelled, I could not wash away the residue from my body or my mind. Ma' knocked on the bathroom door to see if I was all right and told me to open the door. I told her I was fine and begged her not to come in that I just wanted to be alone. Ma' managed to forced the door open and come in. I told her that I was so afraid that, if I came out of what had come to be my safe haven that the rapist would attack me again because, I knew he had not yet been captured and was still out there lurking around somewhere. She hugged me gently, and repeatedly encouraged me not to worry, that everything was going to be alright.

After the raped, my life became different. I didn't want to talk to God anymore and I was not the same happy little girl anymore. Deep down inside, I felt angry, alone, violated, torn, and in severe pain. Emotionally, I didn't want to return to school, I felt unstable, I cried most of the time and was totally paranoid. I wondered what people would be saying about me and the incident and if they believed me. I wanted to crawl into a shell and never come out. But, I had to face the people. I remember when I returned to school, it seemed like the students were all staring and whispering about me. My friends who walked home with me, the day that I was brutally attacked by that strange man, did not even ask me "if I was ok". No one ever said anything to me. Even the teachers stared at me and never tried to comfort me. I was all alone. I walked from class to class by myself. I ate lunch and sat by myself in the cafeteria. I was very much alone. I felt like an out cast as if I was wearing a sign that said **"Beware! Victim! Just raped!"**

Chapter 9

Depression

My grades began to drop. I could not concentrate anymore. I kept thinking, "When are they going to find that man, and suppose he is outside watching me?" I never went down the railroad tracks again. Ma' advised me to walk home down the street where I would be visible and there was the traffic of other people traveling from school and work. Yet I still felt alone with the people around me, but they were not with me. In my subconscious mind, I begin to build a wall of being rejected and shut out. I really found out who my friends were during that time. I would think that people would want to help or talk to you when you are in a dilemma but people really do not want to be bothered with you. Maybe it is because they don't know what to say to you or what to do to help you but I began to think that it was because of association. No one wanted to be associated with me because I had been raped. There were even times I thought people would think that maybe I was lying about what had happened to me or that in some sense I had provoked it. Therefore, as soon as I heard the school bell rang I would get my books, and run out of the school towards home as fast as I could.

I began to blame my mother for what had happened to me. I would often think to myself that if she would have never left us this would never have happened to me. She dropped us off, just left us and kept going. What kind of a mother was she? Why did I have to suffer? God, why me? I thought that you loved me and I was your child. You could have stopped this man. God, why did you not stop him? I had so many questions and no answers. The tears would began to run down my face. My mind began to wander over and over again. It was like the enemy was trying to drive me crazy and make me kill myself. It seemed as if something had

Raped by Man, Saved by God

a strong hold on me. Ma' said that demons will come back seven times seven and that I must pray for God to deliver me from depression and fear.

Constantly I would find myself shutting down. I didn't want to talk to anyone. I did my homework and my chores and sat down quietly not saying a word or wanting anyone to say anything to me. I overheard Da' tell Ma' that he believed she needed to take me to the doctor because I just did not seem right after what had happened to me. I thought maybe Da' thinks that I am going crazy and that I needed some type of mental help. I was starting to believed I needed some help also because I just could not take it anymore. Ma' made an appointment with mental health the next day following their conversation.

When we arrived at mental health and entered the office, the receptionist told us to have a seat. When the door opened the very first person I saw was an African American, short skinny man who was smiling and telling me towards so that he could talk to me. He was a very friendly man but I never understand why I had to have another male talk to me again when I had been raped by a man. I felt like they should have had a woman to speak to me to help me. The doctor began asking me questions about how I felt about men and how did I feel about myself. Every time I went to visit with the doctor at mental health, he would ask what did I want to talk about, my feelings about the rape and how I felt about men in general. I really did not want to discuss my problems with him. Although, he tried to convince me that I should discuss what had happened to me, and talk about my problems, I felt that because he was a man he would never understand how I really felt. He wanted to know if I needed any medicine, to help me sleep? I told him, "No. I did not want to depend on medicine. I never wanted anything to control my life again. The next day I went back to school. While I was in class the principal unexpectedly called my name over the intercom to come to his office. The students all turned around and looked at me as I got up and walked towards the door. I was afraid and wondered what did he want with me.

Chapter 10

The Detectives

When I got to the principal's office there stood two well-dressed white men in black suits and ties. They looked very important. They told me to have a seat, that they wanted to talk to me. The men begin to explain that they were detectives who worked for the police department. They informed me that they had arrested a man who fit the description, he was outside in the car and wanted me to identify him. Fear seeped in, I became scared and wanted to run and hide. I was very nervous, my whole body began to shake and I felt like I was going to pass out. The detectives explained to me that everything would be alright. They told me to take a deep breath and try to relax. I asked the detectives, "Please don't make me go near the man." Instead, I wanted to know if I could just look outside and identify him from there while remaining inside. They said, "Yes."

My heart began to beat faster and my legs were shaking as I walked closer to the door. With each and every step I took it seemed like my legs got weaker and weaker. I asked myself: "Suppose it is not him, maybe they got the wrong man." But when the detectives went to opened the door, a policeman took the man out of the car, he stood there with handcuffs on looking at the door. The blood rushed in my veins, my heart was pounding. As I stood looking out at him, tears began to run, down my face. The detectives asked me, "Is this the man, who raped you?" My voice became silent. They asked me again, "Is this the man, who raped you?" I remembered his face, its one that I will never forget. It was him. I told them "yes, that is him. Thank God, you found him. That is definitely him." The detectives signaled the police officer to put the rapist back in the car and take him to the police department.

The detectives told me that I had to go with them to the

police station and that Ma' would meet us there. I had to sign some papers and make a sworn statement that this was the man who had raped me. On the way to the police station the detective explained to me that another young girl had said this same man had raped her. When I entered the room a young girl was waiting. She had to be about 16 years old, but her body development made her appear to be much older. She seemed nonchalant. She asked me if I had been raped also? I said, "Yes." She said, "are you going to press charges against the man?" I said, "Yes." She told me that she was from New York and that she was returning there. Then she said that she had nothing to say about what had happened. That she was too embarrassed and did not have time to press charges. I could not believe my ears. I asked her, "You were raped but you are not going to press charges against him?" She just seemed so unconcerned. She looked at me and said, "Good luck," as she turned and walked out of the room.

Maybe that is why men continue to get away with rape crimes over and over again because the victims are terrified, scared and afraid to discuss what has happened to them. They continue to commit the same crime because most victims are not willing to come forth and speak up. Someone has to be willing to do something because the cycle has to stop. I had nothing to lie about. It happened and I had the evidence to prove it. I was to committed to testifying. No matter what he must not get away with this again. On one hand, this had to be one of the worst days of my life. On the other hand, I felt truly blessed that God had answered my prayers and the rapist had been caught. One of the detective's opened the door and said, "don't be afraid, everything will be all right." I just held my head down and began to thank God, that they had found the man who had raped me. Ma' was there, she gave me a hug and said, "I knew they would find him."

A police officer came in and directed us to a small room where I had to give my statement and tell what had happened. He advised me that a trial would take place and I would be called to testify. I would have to tell the truth about what had happened to me. He also told me that even though this man had raped the other girl, before me that she would not be testifying. I became so angry because if she had reported this before then this might not had happened to me. He explained to me that testifying would be hard and the prosecutor would ask me a lot of questions that might be very personal and embarrassing on the stand. I did not care because I wanted justice to be done; I was the victim and I would not be terrified anymore. I prayed for God to strengthen me and keep me.

As we left the police department I felt a little relieved knowing that they had found the man and he was detained. Some of my worries left me, but you can never forget what happens to you. My family was very happy that they found the man, and was glad that it was almost over, but this was only the beginning. The man was incarcerated but I knew that the trial would really be hard to endure. I returned to school the next day, trying to focus on my work but it was difficult. I was a different person now, my life had changed and I believed that danger was everywhere, and it did not have a tag on it for any perspective person. No one was trustworthy now to me and I felt as though I had to be constantly watching over my shoulder, especially for men.

I remember the word of God says that you reap what you sow. If you sow bad seeds, you reap bad seeds. I wonder why do bad things happen to good people however, good people are not except from danger, it looks for us. We are all born in sin and no one is perfect. As the days went by I kept wondering when the case would go to trail?

Chapter 11

Leaving Home

I will never forget, it was Thanksgiving Day and the Turkey was smelling good. The family was all talking and listening to music. The TV was on and the fresh smell of food filled the air. We all sat down to dinner, Da' said the grace, we couldn't wait for him to finish the blessing. It was like a race, pass the peas, pass the Turkey, we laughed at the stories Ma' told and deep inside it was great to be alive. After dinner my sister and I washed the dishes and swept the floor. All of a sudden I began to feel dizzy and hot. I ran to the bathroom to throw up, my food came out of me like flowing water. Tears began to run down my face. I wondered what was wrong with me.

Maybe I ate too much, or maybe I was coming down with the flu. I decided to lie down and rest hoping I would feel better tomorrow. But when tomorrow came I still felt sick, my head ached, I felt very dizzy, upset and nauseated. Ma' thought I had the flu, and tried to give me some medicine but I threw it back up. I could not understand what was wrong with me. Maybe Ma' would take me to the doctor to get a flu shot and some more medicine or just get me some help so that I would feel better.

The next day it was Saturday and we had to do our chores. I felt a litter better, but something still was not right, because every time I ate, my food would come back up. One night while lying in the bed, I overhead Ma' talking to my mother. Ma' told her that I was getting sick and that I could not keep anything on my stomach, I was always throwing up my food, that she must make arrangements for me to come to New York. Ma' she would call Uncle Hair, to see if I could get a ride with him to New York. Uncle Hair lived in South Carolina, but traveled to New York every year. I began to cry. I didn't want to leave Ma' because she had been so nice to me. Why would she send me to live with my mother whom I did not know? The next day Ma' started packing my clothes, and kept telling me that things were going to be all right. I kept asking her what was wrong, and why was she sending me away to live in New York. I didn't want to go, I begged her not to make me go, but she told me I had go. She told my sister to ride with me and make sure I get there.

The next day Uncle Hair came to pick us up. The car was a small one and he put my bags in the car. I hugged Ma' and cried, because I felt very much alone. The trip was a long one. It seemed that we drove for hours and hours. I was very tired and, it seem that we hit every bump there was. When we arrived in New York there were tall buildings everywhere. I had never in my life seen anything like it. I was so amazed, and people were everywhere. It reminded me of ants, where there were thousands of them and they all followed each other. The cars and taxicabs raced down the street at high rates of speed, going nowhere fast, rushing you to the other side like maybe telling you to get over or else get hit. Their world was totally different from our world in Carolina. It seemed as if we went from a snails pace to a cheetahs pace in a matter of hours. My sister kept asking

Uncle Hair questions, like what's that and look at that, she was so amazed. We saw kids with the fire hydrant open and playing in the water. I thought that was against the law, but Uncle Hair said it was ok. When we arrived at my mother's apartment there was a lady waiting on the step. She was short and fair completion. I had not seen my mother for years, and she had moles on her face like me. Uncle Bubba said in a loud voice, there is your mother. To me, she was like a stranger. A part of me was happy because she was my mother and another part of me was sad because I did not know her. First she had left me with other people, and next I come to see her with a sickness that I could not explain. I figured that she was not too happy to see me. Maybe I was another problem she had to encountered.

When we got out of the car my legs were stiff and I was tired. My sister jumped out of the car and ran to my mother, she appeared to be so happy, I guess she forgot about the way my mother just left us. My mother hugged my sister and kissed her. Then it was my turn, she hugged and kissed me also and she asked me to go upstairs and wait. I had to walk up a lot of stairs, I looked out of the window and saw

Raped by Man, Saved by God

her talking to Uncle Bubba. I wondered what they were talking about. The apartment was nice and clean, it had two bedrooms, and a day bed. The sickness hit me again, I had to throw up again. I ran to the bath room, and made it just in time. I did not want her mad with me, so I cleaned the bathroom seat off. I wondered if I had contracted a disease from that man or what was wrong with me. My mother came upstairs and asked me to change my clothes, said that we had to take the train to 42nd Street. She never said why, or where we were going. As I changed clothes I notice she was staring at me like she was examining me. I turned around because I was ashamed, and she kept rushing me. She told me that I needed some new clothes and we would go shopping. New clothes that was nice, I never really had that many clothes. She smiled and I smiled back. As we got on the subway the people did not look too friendly. She told me not to stare or not to speak to them, that New York was different from the South. I obeyed her and kept looking ahead. The train shook so you had to hold onto the rails or the poles in the middle of the isles. It was very crowded and you had to hold or you would fall. The people in New York were different.

Tamar Village

They dressed different and looked different. The next stop was ours, my mother told me to stand up so that we could get off the train, quickly.

When we got off the train, we walked it seemed like forever. I thought we would never get there. We arrived at a small building and people were sitting while waiting to see the doctor. The receptionist asked if she could help us. My mother told her that we had an appointment. She asked us to take a seat, that the doctor would be with us soon. I thought the doctor, oh good, my mother is going to get me some help with what ever is wrong with me. The nurse came out to get us, and asked me to go to the exam room next to her office. She asked me to get undressed and put on the robe that hung on the door. I sat on the table waiting for the doctor. When he came in, he introduced himself as Dr. Moore, he was a tall white man, with dark black hair. He looked different like he had Indian in him. He wore a black cap, maybe it was his religion. Dr. Moore said he was going to run a series of tests to try to find out what was wrong with me. I had to urinate in a cup next, as I laid on the exam table waiting for the doctor to examine me, it reminded me of a horse stable.

There were two places you had to put your feet. The doctor held this instrument that looked like a duck bill, it was plastic and big. I thought to myself, I know he is not going to insert that in me. He explained that it would not hurt and I should simply try to relax my body by taking several deep breaths. It felt very uncomfortable, but it did not last long. Whenever he finished he advised me to put my clothes back on, and he would speak to my mother. He spoke to my mother, we left and went back home.

Chapter 12

The Child Within

When we arrived home my mother asked me to sit down, that she needed to talk to me. She began to say that sometimes things happen and we don't know why, but it happens. She explained that the reason I was getting sick was because I was pregnant by the rapist, and that it was too late to get an abortion because I was too far along. She explained that Ma' thought that I was pregnant, but didn't believe in abortion, and that was why she sent me to New York. When she said that, I ran in the bathroom and closed the door, I fell to the floor and began to cry, I wanted to kill myself. I became so angry and hurt, tears just ran down my face. Why me, why did this have to happen? I cried and begged my mother not to let me have this child. I can not have a child, I'm just a child myself, I had to finish school, and one day go to college.

My mother asked me to please come out of the bathroom. I just wanted to run away and never come back. I hated myself for walking down the railroad track, maybe if I had walked another way, this would have never happened. The pain was too much to bear, I was raped and now I'm pregnant. This had to be a dream. I wanted to wake up so it would all go away. I later cried myself to sleep, when I woke up my sister stood looking at me crying in disbelief, wondering also why did this happen. My head began to hurt, and I felt sick all over again. There was a man in the kitchen that my mother introduced as her husband. It was my stepfather and he shook my hand and said that if I needed anything he would help me. I never wanted to trust a man again, the fear was a fear of anger and hurt. I just nodded my head and kept walking. Later something began to happen to my body.

I notice my body changing, my breasts began to get bigger. My weight began to increase and my stomach was beginning to get larger. I hated the way I looked, I was ashamed and could not go outside because I was afraid of what people would say. My confidence was like a dog that had been abused and was afraid of getting hurt again.

What would they think, a child having a child. When I had my doctor's appointment, people stared at me and whispered but I would just hold my head down. The nurse was very friendly, I guess they knew what happened and tried to make me feel better. The nurse explained to me that I was four months pregnant, and in five months the baby would be born. The nurse said that I would be going to a class for unwed mothers and, they would teach me how to take care of my child. She advised me that I should not be afraid, that there were other mothers in the class who never had a child and would be going through the same thing.

In class they taught us how to take care of our bodies after having a baby, I would go to class every month, then as time got closer to have the baby, I would go every week. They taught us the symptoms and effects of postpartum syndrome, and the need of a support system if you still needed help. She asked me if I had a name for the baby, and I said no. I had not given it much thought, despite the fact the baby was soon to come. She wanted me to name the baby Samuel. I was really scared to have a baby, I had heard that it hurt, and sometimes women died during child birth.

One Sunday morning I was in the kitchen washing dishes and I notice something strange was happening inside of me, I felt a movement like waves going across the TV. I ran to my mother to tell her something was happening, she smiled and said, that's the baby, he was awake, and there is life inside of you now. I did not know what to say about the life inside of me. I did not know how I should feel. He was a part of me, and another part was the man who raped me. Instead of being happy, I became depressed. When I laid down at night the baby would move and sometimes it felt like a knot, it would be so uncomfortable that I could not rest. I wanted him to stop moving, to be still, but sometimes it appeared that he didn't care. I began to get bigger and my mother brought me maternity clothes, and new shoes because my feet began to swell and hurt. My stomach started to itch from the stretch marks, my mother gave me lotions to rub with to help sooth the itch. I realized my mother was a nice caring lady, and that she did love me. I wondered how it would have been living with my mother.

My mother tried to make it as comfortable for me as she could. My sister remained in New York with me, I knew she wanted to live with my mother. At that time I really did not like New York, I wanted to be with ma' again, I missed her and Da'. They were the only parents that I knew. My mother was like a stranger to me. I loved her but I never really knew her, and she didn't know me. We never had much to talk about. I helped around the house and did my best to stay busy.

Ma' would call me every now and then to ask me how was I doing, and if I liked New York? I told her that I missed her, and would be glad to see her. I explained to her that Annabella, my sister, was not coming back to live with us. She wanted to stay with my mother and had already enrolled in school. She would be going to an all girl school. She seemed to like it, and many days I watched her as she left for school, I was so jealous of my sister because she had a normal life, and my life was ruined, it was not fair. I kept asking myself, why did this happen to me, and what was the reason for it?

My sister got new school clothes and didn't have to go to church any more. My mother was not a religious woman, she went to church sometimes but not as much as Ma' used to make us go. My sister was allowed to wear her dresses shorter, go to games and to the school dances. Ma' would never have allowed that. Our focus while we were with Ma' was God. Annabella was now free as a bird.

Chapter 13

The Birth

The day was November 8, 1969 and that day my back began to hurt, unbearably. I screamed for my mother. It was an excruciating pain that felt as if someone hit me in the back with a ton of bricks, all I could do was bend over at my knees and hope the pain would cease. The pain and the pressure was so grave that I felt like I had to use the bathroom. Then I remembered the breathing techniques we had learned in class and begin to take short, rapid, deep breaths. The pain would subside for a few moments and then come back each time stronger that the one before. My mother called the ambulance and told them I was in labor, gave them the address, to come and take me to the hospital. Although, it only took them a few minutes to get to our house, it seemed like an eternity. Once they put me into the ambulance, we were on our way to the hospital, it was time for me to have my baby. The ambulance did not use the flashing light and sirens on the way to the hospital, I guess we had time, but I wondered why they did not turn them on to get the people out of the way so we could hurry and get there, the sooner we got there the sooner this would be over with.

When we arrived at the hospital they took me off of the stretcher and put me in a wheel chair. The nurse wheeled me upstairs and advised me to continue the breathing process. I told her that the pains were coming more often and were more severe. The nurse helped me to get undressed and said the doctor would be in soon. The pains were getting worse and worse. This had to be the most horrible pain for anyone to endure. I began to cry and I begged my mother not to leave me.

The doctor entered the room with his scrubs on. I had seen this on TV, but this was real. His face was covered with a mask, and he began to put on some gloves. He picked up an instrument that looked like an oversized needle, told me to sit up, this was not going to hurt but, I should not move. The doctor said this would ease the pain and I would not feel anything after he gave me the shot, but the key was not to budge.

Then the doctor injected the medicine into my back and a few moments later the pain was gone. He informed me that I had dilated ten centimeters and that all I had to do was to push when he coached me to do so, I tried to push, but nothing happened. He said, "push, push, keep pushing," I gave one big final push and all of a sudden I heard a loud sound of a cry, the doctor announced "it's a boy".

I hate to say it but I was not happy at all. I was just glade that it was over with. The nurse brought the baby around for to me to see him, but I really did not want to look at the baby. Should I not be happy and joyous that I just had a baby boy? Therefore, when she showed me the baby, I turned my head very fast after I looked at him because I had no feelings at all. How could I accept a child that was the product of a crime of violence and dispassionate behavior? The nurse wanted to name him, I told her that would be fine she did, and he was named Samuel. It was mandatory to stay in the hospital for at least 3 days after giving birth before I could go home. On the third day, my mom and stepfather came to bring us home from the hospital. When we arrived home my sister was at the door to greet us and get the first chance to hold the baby. Once we got settled in I learned how hard it was trying to taking care of a baby. I asked my mother if we could give the baby up for adoption, she said "yes, but we had to take the baby to trial to show the court, as a result of the rape." Later that day, Ma' called and said that the trial was on the following Friday, and that we needed to be there. I thought bringing the baby to trial was so embarrassing, why did I need to bring him? Why could I not leave the baby in New York with my mother?

That was a hard week for me. Fear overwhelmed me once again, I felt all alone and had no one to talk to about how I felt. I was getting up at night feeding the baby, and wishing he would stop crying, something he seemed to do a lot. I had so much resentment, that this was not my fault, and why was I suffering. Why did I have to tell people that

Raped by Man, Saved by God

I had a child at 15 years old, when I was really just a child myself. I hated that I had become a woman at 15, bearing a child, that the little girl inside of me was gone, and I had to portray a woman at an early age. It was not fun being a mother, with the responsibilities of taking care of a child it was breathtaking, I was tired everyday. I had to wash his clothes, wash my clothes, feed him, give him a bath, watch after him and try to keep my sanity. It's amazing how one day your life is comfortable, and the next day your life is in complete turmoil. You never know what is going to happen to you in life, or how it will come. Deep inside I kept telling myself that I must be strong, I must testify in court so that this man would not ruin anyone else's life.

My mother and stepfather had to work and my sister went to school, so there were many days I was home alone with the baby, feeling sorry for myself. I would often wonder what the outcome of the trial would be. What kind of questions they would ask me and who the jury would believe. When my mother came home I made sure dinner was cooked and the house was clean. My mother was trying to be there for me, but something was missing. I guess I had built up a wall and did not want anyone to come in. I did not want anyone to talk to me, I did not want to be touched or held. I learned that people try to pacify you by telling you things are going to be alright, it's going to be ok, but they do not know what you are really feeling, unless they have experienced your situation. How can something be alright, when it has already happened? The realization will never make it be alright. I had been violated, I was the victim and I wanted justice.

Friday, the day for me to travel back to North Carolina had come and it was a sad day. I had to leave my mother and sister behind. My sister seemed happy because she was with my mother, and she wanted to develop a closeness with her. That morning I packed my clothes and the baby's clothes, I said good-by to my stepfather as my mother called the taxi to come and pick us up to take us to the airport. My mother rode with us but did not say much while riding to the airport. I felt alone again, like when she left us the first time. But deep inside I felt stronger. Being angry will drive your determination. When I began to board the airplane, my mother began to cry and said that if I needed her to please call. Could she not see and did she not know that I needed her at a time like this. Yes, I needed her, but what could she do. When you are raped, the first person to help you should be your mother. I was upset with her deep inside but I had too much on my plate to worry about if I needed her. The only person I needed at that time was God. I needed Him to give me the strength I needed to get through this. I was mad inside with my mother but deep inside I knew that she had to work, and could not go with me.

As we boarded the airplane, I was afraid because this was the first time I had ever flown on an airplane. The flight attendant looked at me and smiled, but no one really said much to me. I just wanted to hurry and get back home. I took my seat, had a short nap and awoke a little while later to the pilot saying that "we are getting ready to land, please fasten your set belts". My stomach began to turn and I felt nauseated. The landing was fast and rough, but thank God, we landed.

When I got off the plane, I saw someone waving. It was Ma' and her husband. She grabbed the baby as soon as I got off the plane and kissed me. I could tell she was happy to see me. I felt that she loved children and that is why she kept us. She began to tell me that I had to needed to get back in school so that I could finish, and that she would keep the baby. I was stunned, keep the baby! I did not want that baby! How could she want to keep a baby whose father had raped me and one that I definitely did not want. I just looked at her, she kept talking not seeming to understand how I felt. It seemed that no one actually cared how I felt. I wanted to say please don't keep the baby but I was taught never to talk back to grown-ups. Something heavy came over me and I wanted to shut down. My mind began to wonder why me, where was God and why did this happen to me? When men came around our house, I wanted to run and hide. They became the enemies in my mind and my mind began to talk to me. It seemed as if I heard two people holding a conversation. I would lay in bed at night and cry. I became depressed and lonely. People surrounded me, but it was like they were not there. When people would ask me if that was my baby I would tell them no. I was in denial, and the hurt and pain became harder and harder to bear.

Da' told Ma' that I needed to get help, because he noticed

that I seemed distant again. Ma' rescheduled an appointment for me to see a doctor. When I arrived there, the counselor began asking me questions. I was immediately put on guard, because it was that man again, and I did not want to speak to him. Secondly, I felt that the questions he asked me were crazy. I did not want to be there, all I really wanted to do was go home.

The next day Ma' enrolled me back into school, and told me that she would keep the baby. Some of the students at school would be whispering about me and I felt bad not knowing what they were saying. I did not want anyone to know that I had a child, I did not have many friends and really did not want any, I really felt like a hermit. It was hard to study and concentrate on my school work knowing that I had to go to court soon. Sometimes, I would find myself day dreaming wondering what it would be like if this had never happened. I always wanted to be an artist, but not now. I felt that something had stopped my dream. Sometimes I would fall asleep in class because of having to get up with the baby at night. Often I was physically tired from the night before to concentrate as I would have otherwise.

One day a friend was visiting our house and made the comment, "you are a woman now". I wanted to just scream and run away, I was not a woman, I was still a child. Just because I had, a child did not make me a woman, the only thing was that I had lost my virginity. The dictionary states that a woman is a girl grown up, an adult, a married woman, a woman of high ideals, I was none of these. I was still a girl, which means a child from birth to age eighteen. I noticed the way he looked at me, and wondered if he would have tried to touched me, I believe I would have killed him. Men had become my worst enemies, I hated them and never wanted them near me again.

I was always protective of myself. It was like I had a shield up, and you could not get in. I had never read a love story but I was sure that love was totally different from this. I never knew that pain was so scary and it affects someone so very deeply. I felt that the pain I had endured had cut me to the core of my soul and that scare would never go away or completely heal. I believed that it would be there for the rest of my life. The sound of the word rape made me angry, I hated to hear that word, it felt bad, it sounded bad, and it left a bad taste in my mouth. This was no different from the bible days, II Samuel; "Amnon's sin against Tamar", when Amnon raped his sister. He had commented a sin and God was angry.

Chapter 14

The Trial

The next week it was time for the trial to start. Ma and I had an appointment to meet with my lawyer at the court house the Friday before trial. I prayed every night for God to give me the strength to endure. I had never forgotten God because he did save my life and I still loved him, but I was confused and had mixed emotions. That Thursday night before, I remember falling asleep just repeating in my mind over and over again, "Lord help me, Lord help me". Early Friday morning I was awakened by the birds singing, and the smell of breakfast cooking. I got up to go to the bathroom to take a bath, to get ready to go to the court room for the first time, fear came upon me again and my legs began to shake, but I kept speaking to myself saying be strong it is almost over. Ma' of course, was already up, and that breakfast sure did smell good. She told me to hurry and get dressed, so that I would have time to eat, that the lawyer would be expecting us by 9:00 a.m. and we did not want to be late.

When we arrived the attorney came and introduced himself and advised me that he would be helping me to put this man in jail for life. He tried to explain to us what to expect, and told us where everyone would be sitting. He told me, being that I was a young teenage girl some of the questions that the prosecutor will ask me will not be nice because it was his job to try to discredit or blemish my character, but to try to answer them to the best of my ability.

He said that the defense attorney's job was to try to keep his client from going to jail. In the courtroom he pointed out that the two male witnesses would be setting in the chairs next to me, the jury would be sitting in the jury box but to not let that frighten me. Just look straight ahead and answer the questions. The jury's job was to make sure the man had a fair trial and decide who was telling the truth. He said if I felt that I did not understand the questions, to ask the attorney to repeat himself.

He advised me that there would be no one there to assist me with answering the questions, but to answer them to the best of my knowledge and if I needed to take a deep breath, do so, relax and start over. I was also informed that there would be spectators, news reporters, his family members and mine as well, in the courtroom. I was not to focus on them, but on the questions that the defense attorney asked, and to be honest. He said that the trial would probably last about a week, and that I should get plenty of rest and sleep.

My heart beat was faster than ever. Mentally, I felt much stronger, because I wanted to put this man away for life so that he would not hurt or harm anyone else. But physically, I felt my body wanting to shut down, because of the shame, quilt, embarrassment and the emotional roller coaster I felt like I was on. Tears began to run down my face, and I had a flash back of the past with confusion trying to take over my mind. However, I stood strong and refused to give in. I fight daily with my past, it's something that never goes away.

When the attorney finished explaining the procedure, he asked if I had any questions, I said "no."

Ma' asked me if I was alright, I replied "yes mam", she said "stay strong and hold on just a little while longer, this too shall pass." It was a very frightening time in my life and no one knows how you feel until they have walked in your shoes.

Over the weekend, I became very nervous and lost my ability to eat. It seemed as if I had knots in my stomach, but I had to convince myself that I could do this. That weekend I prayed to God to give me the strength, and to help me when I felt powerless. The night before the trial, I could not sleep, I tossed and turned in bed thinking of the trial and what they might say, wondering who would be in the court room and would his family be there. My sister slept with me and told me to be still and to move over. It seemed as if when I finally fell asleep, it was time to get up, waking up again to the smell of ma" cooking ham, grits, and eggs. When I went into the kitchen ma' smiled and said, "this is your big day, when you get your chance to tell what happened to you, I want you to get up there and just tell the honest truth." She said, "the truth will out weigh a lie every time, and when you swear on the bible that means you have to tell the truth because God will strike you down if you lie." Ma' never believed in telling lies, she said God did not like a liar. Ma' said don't let the people in there make you afraid, hold your head up, be strong and of good cheer God will protect you." I wondered why God had not protected me from this man, but I kept thinking, at least I am alive.

I wondered what to wear. We did not have that many clothes and I only had three Sunday dresses for church. Ma' told me to wear my blue skirt and white blouse we wore to sing in the choir. As time came close for us to leave to go to court I felt my self-esteem going down, I dressed slowly and walked slowly with my head held down, Ma' said "hold your head up baby, you are somebody." My brother and sister looked at me with sadness in their eyes as if to say, "take care and hurry back". As we walked out the door, I was overwhelmed with a flood gate of tears. I had an uneasy feeling, today I would be facing the enemy who made me a victim and thought he had gotten away.

As we got out of the car with the baby at the courthouse, people were everywhere, trying to see him. I covered and wrapped him up so no one could see his face. We had to push our way through the crowd to the courthouse through a side door to escape the press and news reporters. We walked upstairs, I saw two men, and remembered they were the ones God had sent to save my life. I wanted to hug them, but I kept my distance and kept looking ahead. My attorney asked me to sit and wait because the trial would begin in about 10 minutes. He asked if I was alright, and how was the baby? The baby was introduced as being the child of a victim as evidence from the results of the rape. My legs began to shake and I felt sick again, as I sat and waited. Then the attorney opened the door and said, "It's your turn, you must be strong, look straight ahead, don't look at him. You must put your hands on the Bible and tell the truth, the whole truth, and nothing but the truth. As I walked into the room, I saw people everywhere, I felt weak but I kept looking straight ahead. I saw the jurors; they were men and women, white and black. I raised my right hand and swore I would tell the truth and the whole truth. As I sit in the chair, I could not help but notice all the people in the court room and the rapist sitting over there looking like the cat that ate the canary and was going to get away with it. I hated to look at him. His expressions were intimidating, but I was not going to hide the truth about him raping me. I noticed people whispering and pointing as I told my story. I felt that he must pay for what he had done. I heard that he had a wife and two children, but I did not care, I just wanted it to be over.

His attorney approached me and began questioning me. His first questions were if I had ever been to the boy's dorms at the University because that was the local college by the railroad track that I had to pass everyday to get home, and did I have a boyfriend? I answered, "no sir." He said "was your mother so strict that she would not let you date, so you became pregnant by a boy in college, and now you are trying to say that this man raped you?" I answered "no sir." The attorney's voice became loud, he talked as if he was mad and that I was lying to him, I started crying, tears began to run down my face, my nose was running, and I was frightened. I noticed the man that raped me was smiling like this was a game, and he was going to win. Something inside of me became strong and angry that he had the nerve to smile after what he had done. My tears began to dry up, and a power came over me that I could not explain. I had found renewed strength from deep within me to fight. As if a voice was saying he will not win this time, I will not let you rape or hurt anyone else the way you have hurt me. You should have killed me when you had me, but I will not be afraid of you again. I dried my tears, told every detail and did not leave anything out. I told how he dragged me into the woods and told me to shut up. I explained that he had a knife, and how he said that he would kill me if I tried to get away. Courage rose up inside of me and I began to fight back with words and power. I will not be ashamed or violated again. I explained how he was hiding in the path, waiting for the first victim that came by, and how he came out of the path to claim what he thought was his, taking a part of me that one day should have belonged to my husband. He acted like a wild animal that was hunting for food, smelling like the scent of something foul, and possessed with the spirit of lust. I did not feel afraid anymore, God answered my prayers, he had given me strength to endure and it was working. As I walked down from the stand, Ma" looked at me, smiled and said "you did great, I am so proud of you.

My attorney told me that the witnesses would testify the next day. The rapist also had witnesses to say that he was with them the day that the rape took place, but it was a lie and the truth would unfold. Justice would be done. I felt that I did not have to worry, that prayer and God would do the rest. When I arrived home after the day in court I became very upset and couldn't sleep that night, and my mind began to play tricks on me. As I lie in bed I could hear Ma' praying for me. She prayed loud and strong, her voice echoed against the walls, and I knew God had to hear her. Her cry was like a cry in the wilderness saying Lord hear my cry.

The next morning I had to go to court again. It was tough having to go everyday looking into the face of the man that raped me. The people set in the courtroom concentrating, the jury kept looking as if they were trying to figure out what actually happened. There were four women and six men and they had to make the right decision, whether to send him to jail or let him go. I asked God to prevail in this situation, for justice to be done, and to prevent him from raping anyone else. I felt that the men on the jury thought that I was lying, and the women thought I was telling the truth. I felt that the women could relate because we have that womanly instinct. Men can also be hurt and get raped too, but they don't always reveal those encounters simply because they have to portrait that macho image. But we all are held responsible and have to give an account for everything that we do. The last day of the trial had finally come and the verdict would be read. I was really worried as to what the outcome would be, but Ma' told me to get some rest and try not to worry.

Chapter 15

The Verdict

Morning came and we got up early so that we could pray and ask God for the victory, and whatever decision was made, we would give God the glory. We did not talk much that morning, it was so quite you could hear a pin drop. As I dressed the baby and put my clothes on, we had breakfast and I waited until Da' started the car. We had to be there by 8:30 a.m. When we arrived, the courtroom was already full. I noticed people standing around looking and staring some were looking mean and hateful and others were fairly pleasant. Again, they were trying to see the baby but I covered his face as we rushed into the courtroom. One reporter was, trying to ask us questions and take our picture, but my attorney just replied "no comment." Today was like a circus that I did not want to be in. In life there are things that happen that are beyond our ability to control, we do not always choose the paths in our lives, however, sometimes things just happen. We can still fight because we have our rights, and because this is the land of the free.

I was very nervous, my stomach was in knots, and my head had stared to hurt. I figured it was anxiety that came over me, since today the sentencing would be read. My mind began to wonder, what if he goes free, then justice would not prevail, and if he does get time in prison, then all my efforts and existence had not been in vain. The Bible says that vengeance is mine said the Lord and I will repay. Today I would see if the Lord would repay. I was only there to say what had happened to me, it was God who would give the sentence. The Bible says "Do not be afraid of the terror that come by night nor the arrow that flieth by day, nor the pestilence that walketh in darkness; nor for the destruction that wasteth at noonday. Only with thine eyes shalt thou behold and see the reward of the wicked." (Psalm 91) I have always loved to read Psalm 91 for God is a refuge and a fortress. Whatever happened to me God did give his Angels charge over me because he will keep me in all thy ways.

As we entered the courtroom, the rapist family was on one side and mine was on the other. You could feel the tension about the decision that the jury would make. As I glanced at my attacker, I wondered how he felt knowing what he did was wrong, knowing that he might go to jail for a long time, but he seemed to show no remorse, he just sat there like he did not have a care in the world. His family members looked at me with revulsion if to say he was innocent and why would you do this to him? As I sat waiting for the verdict, I looked at Ma', she just smiled and said "it will be ok."

The Judge came into the courtroom and the Sheriff asked us to stand as he announced the judge. The jury entered the courtroom from another door. The judge asked the jury if they had reached the verdict. The foreman stood and replied "we have." They gave the verdict to the Judge to be announced, my heart was beating so fast. The Judge announced that the jury had made a decision, he asked the man to stand and said, "that on behalf of the state of North Carolina the

Defendant is found Guilty of Rape in the First Degree, that he engaged in vaginal intercourse with a victim who is a child at least 14 years of age, with force on a person against their will and displayed a dangerous weapon to inflict serious personal injury on the victim. This is a Class B1 Felony." The Judge asked the now convicted rapist if he had anything to say, he said "no." The Judge said by the power invested in me for the crime that you have committed, you will be sentence to 20 years to life in prison. When the verdict was given all I could say "Thank you God, Thank you God, Thank you God," justice had prevailed. This brought closure to that part of my life. However, I will always remember what happened to me. The scare will always be there, but I have learned to move on with my life. I have also learned that the past is behind me and God said to not look at the things behind but to focus on the present. No matter what happens to me, God is still in control. Even though ***I was Raped by Man, I was saved by God,*** the author and finisher of my faith.

I do not want to leave you in suspense about what happened to Samuel. I had a healing process to go through. I learned to love my son because he was a part of me. At the age of three, we learned that Samuel was born deaf. I learned to interpret for the deaf so that I could communicate with him. He finished school and is now married. He designed the cover for this book. The devil meant it for evil but God meant it for my good. Interpreting has helped me to relay to the hearing impaired that there is a God that loves us all more than we will ever know.

Made in the USA
Middletown, DE
27 April 2019